Clarkson Public Library
Phone (402) 892-3235

WAR PROTESTERS

By Christopher Schafer

VISIT US AT
WWW.ABDOPUB.COM

Published by ABDO & Daughters, an imprint of ABDO Publishing Company, 4940 Viking Drive, Suite 622, Edina, Minnesota 55435. Copyright ©2004 by Abdo Consulting Group, Inc. International copyrights reserved in all countries. No part of this book may be reproduced in any form without written permission from the publisher.

Printed in the United States.

Edited by: Tamara L. Britton and Kate A. Conley
Graphic Design: Arturo Leyva, David Bullen
Cover Design: Castaneda Dunham, Inc.
Photos: AP/Wide World, Corbis

Library of Congress Cataloging-in-Publication Data

Schafer, Christopher.
   War protesters / Christopher Schafer.
    p. cm.--(War in Iraq)
    Includes bibliographical references and index.
   Summary: Explores why some people believe that the 2003 war against Iraq was unjust and illegal, and how they exposed their beliefs through marches, demonstrations, vigils, and other acts of protest.
    ISBN 1-59197-500-X
    1. Iraq War, 2003--Protest movements--Juvenile literature. [1. Iraq War, 2003--Protest movements.] I. Title. II. Series.

DS79.76 .S33 2004
956.7044`3--dc21
                                        2003051929

TABLE OF CONTENTS

The Highway of Death was the site of much destruction during the Persian Gulf War.

ROOTS OF THE CONFLICT

onflict, especially war, has always spurred tremendous emotion. Operation Iraqi Freedom was no different. Though the war began in 2003, the United States and Iraq had a strained relationship for decades. In August 1990, Iraq invaded and annexed its neighbor Kuwait. Iraq's government had long believed that Kuwait was actually part of Iraq. It thought the military actions were justified. The United Nations (UN), however, disagreed.

Shortly after the annexation, the UN called for Iraqi forces to leave Kuwait by January 15, 1991, or face military force. Iraqi forces refused to leave, and the Persian Gulf War began on January 16, 1991. Troops from the United States and other nations battled the Iraqis to liberate Kuwait. Six weeks later, Iraq's forces had been destroyed and the war was over.

Though the war had ended, Iraq still had to face the consequences of its aggressive actions. The UN imposed sanctions and forbade Iraq from having weapons of mass destruction. It sent weapons inspectors to Iraq to make sure the nation was complying. Often, Iraqi officials refused to cooperate with the weapons inspectors, causing tension between Iraq and UN members.

Then on September 11, 2001, everything changed. That day terrorists from the group al-Qaeda attacked the United States, killing thousands of Americans. U.S. president George W. Bush began a war on terrorism. Though Iraq was not directly involved in the attack, Bush believed that Iraq's dictator, Saddam Hussein, had ties to terrorist groups, including al-Qaeda. He also believed that Saddam Hussein was hiding weapons of mass destruction.

The combination of terrorist ties and weapons of mass destruction made Iraq a worldwide threat. The Bush administration took its concerns to the UN, and in November 2002 it passed Resolution 1441. It warned Iraq would have to pay serious consequences if it did not prove it had destroyed its weapons of mass destruction. Weapons inspectors said that Iraq was not complying with the resolution and asked for more time to resolve the issue peacefully.

Bush, however, believed that the problem was serious and wanted action quickly. But many UN members were adamant

After the terrorist attacks on New York City on September 11, 2001,
U.S. president George W. Bush promised to launch a war against terrorism.

about avoiding a war. France promised to veto any new UN resolution that authorized the use of force. It had strong support from its neighbor, Germany. French president Jacques Chirac told the media that France and Germany had the same point of view regarding the Iraqi crisis. Both nations believed that war should be avoided. "As far as we're concerned, war always means failure," said Chirac. Both nations believed that the decision to go to war was the choice of the UN alone.

Like France, Russia also wanted to veto any new UN resolution authorizing force in Iraq. Russian president Vladimir Putin believed the weapons inspectors needed more time in Iraq and that any attack was unnecessary. He believed that diplomatic measures needed to continue. Likewise, China wanted to see the conflict resolved peacefully. "The Chinese side still supports using political means to resolve the Iraq issues. The door of peace should not be closed," said China's president Jiang Zemin.

Other world leaders also disagreed with the use of force. Pope John Paul II was another powerful opponent of war. Though the pope doesn't control any country's government, he leads the Roman Catholic Church. Many of the world's 1 billion Catholic followers listen to what he says. The pope

WAR PROTESTERS

repeatedly spoke out against the possible war in Iraq. He said that war was "always a defeat for humanity."

The pope believed that coalition forces needed to think about the consequences of the war. He arranged meetings with several world leaders to discuss solving the problems without violence. He even sent important church officials to meet with Saddam and Bush in hopes the conflict could be resolved peacefully.

Despite the opposition Bush faced, he also had allies in his quest to disarm Iraq quickly. Bush's strongest supporter was British prime minister Tony Blair. Blair, like Bush, believed Saddam had illegal weapons that should be destroyed. He supported the use of weapons inspectors in Iraq. When the weapons inspectors left and the war began, however, Blair stood by his American ally. He ordered thousands of British troops to the Middle East to wage war on Iraq.

Another of Bush's supporters was Spanish president José María Aznar. As a member of the European Union (EU), Spain had an important voice in world politics. Aznar believed it was the duty of the EU and the UN to fight terrorism. He told reporters that Spain's cooperation with the United States was total. Bush also drew strong support from

Australian prime minister John Howard. Australia committed fighter jets, warships, and 2,000 troops to the war effort. Howard firmly believed that the war was legal, saying it "has a sound legal basis in the resolutions of the UN Security Council that have already been passed."

These countries, and several others, made up a group known as the Coalition of the Willing. These countries supported the use of military force to remove Saddam from power if he did not comply with UN weapons inspections. Each of these countries contributed to the coalition in a different way. Countries such as the United States, the United Kingdom, and Australia committed military support. Other countries offered funding and the use of bases to launch attacks.

When Bush and his allies failed to receive the UN's approval for an attack, they chose to move forward on their own. On March 17, 2003, President Bush issued Saddam Hussein and his sons an ultimatum: leave Iraq within 48 hours or face a military conflict. Saddam refused to leave, and the war began on March 19, 2003.

WAR PROTESTERS

COALITION OF THE WILLING

The Coalition of the Willing includes 49 countries. These countries are:

Afghanistan

Albania

Angola

Australia

Azerbaijan

Bulgaria

Colombia

Costa Rica

The Czech Republic

Denmark

Dominican Republic

El Salvador

Eritrea

Estonia

Ethiopia

Georgia

Honduras

Hungary

Iceland

Italy

Japan

Kuwait

Latvia

Lithuania

Macedonia

Marshall Islands

Micronesia

Mongolia

The Netherlands

Nicaragua

Palau

Panama

The Philippines

Poland

Portugal

Romania

Rwanda

Singapore

Slovakia

Solomon Islands

South Korea

Spain

Tonga

Turkey

Uganda

Ukraine

The United Kingdom

The United States

Uzbekistan

WHY PROTEST?

During the months leading up to the war, it seemed everyone had an opinion about how the conflict should be resolved. Some people believed that the war was necessary, because they believed that Saddam Hussein was a threat to other nations. Other people believed that there were not enough reasons to justify the war. They wanted the United States and its allies to continue pursuing peaceful options.

Some people had such a strong opinion on whether the war was right or wrong that they demonstrated to support their cause. Most of the people who demonstrated were antiwar protesters. They thought the war was wrong and even illegal, because it did not comply with the UN. They believed the UN was the only group with the power to authorize force. And they were upset that UN weapons inspectors would have to stop their work and leave Iraq, because coalition forces were going to attack.

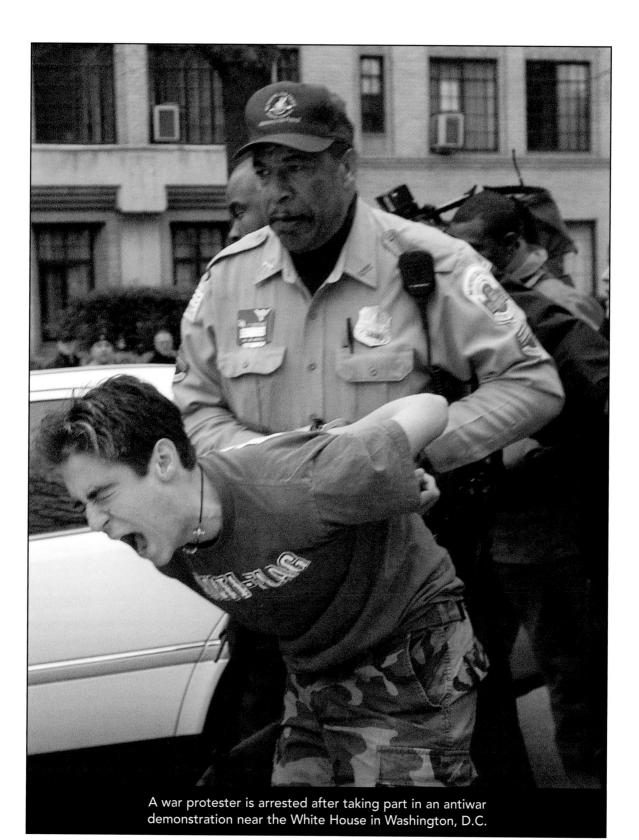

A war protester is arrested after taking part in an antiwar demonstration near the White House in Washington, D.C.

Opponents of the war also argued that there was no proof that Iraq had any relationship with al-Qaeda, and they worried that attacking Iraq would only increase terrorist attacks against the United States. To gain support, the Bush administration tried to make the connection clear. When speaking to the Senate Intelligence Committee, CIA director George Tenet said, "Iraq has, in the past, provided training in document forgery and bomb-making to al-Qaeda. It has also provided training in poisons and gases to two al-Qaeda associates." Despite this, Saddam denied any connection between Iraq and al-Qaeda. "If we had a relationship with al-Qaeda and we believed in this relationship, we wouldn't be ashamed to admit it," said Saddam.

Opponents of the war also believed that the United States was attacking Iraq to gain control of the country's vast oil reserves. The United States uses more oil than any other country, and it does not have enough to supply itself. Iraq, on the other hand, has the second-largest oil reserve in the world. War critics believed that the United States waged war on Iraq to control this oil, or to set up a new Iraqi government that would sell oil to the United States at a lower rate.

WAR PROTESTERS

War protesters also questioned the costs of the war, in terms of both money and human lives. They believed that many civilians and soldiers would die in the war. Some people also believed that the money spent on a war with Iraq could be used in the United States for health care, housing, education, or other social issues instead.

Participants in a "Stop Wars for Oil" peace rally form a human peace sign.

AMERICA RESPONDS

The right to protest is permitted under the First Amendment to the U.S. Constitution. The First Amendment grants people freedom of speech and the right to assemble peaceably. So even before the war began, some people began publicly voicing their opinions against it. They hoped that if they showed support for peace, they could stop the war.

In the months before the war, Americans also began holding many antiwar protests. Usually protesters marched in groups. They used their numbers as a sign of strength for their cause. During these marches, protesters carried signs that showed their feelings about the issue. They also chanted slogans and sang songs of opposition. These actions were designed not only to voice their beliefs on the war, but also to unify the group itself.

One of the largest protests before the war began occurred in Washington, D.C., on January 18, 2003. A group called

Act Now to Stop War and End Racism (ANSWER) organized this march. Organizers estimated that about 500,000 protesters participated. This made it the largest antiwar rally in Washington, D.C., since the Vietnam War.

The protesters met at the Mall and then marched through the streets of Washington, D.C. They listened to speeches from religious leaders such as the Reverend Jesse Jackson, and lawmakers such as U.S. representative John Conyers Jr. Similar marches were also held that day in other U.S. cities.

On March 20, the day after the war in Iraq began, protesters took to the streets to show their disapproval. Approximately 500 cities across the nation held antiwar rallies and peace vigils. People also protested by performing acts of civil disobedience. For example, 10,000 protesters in Chicago blocked traffic by marching down Lake Shore Drive, one of Chicago's busiest streets. Meanwhile, in San Francisco protesters were arrested for sitting in the middle of busy intersections.

The acts of civil disobedience continued as the war progressed. In New York City on March 27, 2003, a coalition of antiwar groups called M27 staged a die-in on a busy street in New York City. They laid in the street to represent the Iraqis who were dying in the war. They also chanted "The people, united, will stop this war." The die-in protest blocked traffic, so police officers were forced to act. They used plastic handcuffs to arrest about 215 protesters.

Not everyone who demonstrated was against the war. In fact, several pro-war rallies also took place in cities across the United States. At these rallies, people sang patriotic songs and waved American flags. Pro-war demonstrators said their marches were to support the nation's troops. "Whether you agree or disagree with the war, it's so important that we send a message to the troops that we stand behind them," said one marcher at a Rally for America in Cleveland, Ohio.

In Toronto, Canada, about 1,000 people also marched to show their support for the United States and its efforts in Iraq. They held a Friends of America rally on April 4, 2003. Stephen Harper, head of the Canadian Alliance, thanked the crowd for "saying to our friends in the United States of America, you are our ally, our neighbor, and our best friend in the whole wide world."

A group of demonstrators stage an antiwar protest.

BOOKS NOT BOMBS

Adults were not the only people voicing their opinion on the conflict in Iraq. In fact, students made up a large and passionate group of protesters. One of the most vocal student organizations was the National Youth and Student Peace Coalition (NYSPC). It was founded after the terrorist attacks of September 11, 2001.

The group condemned the terrorist attacks, but it did not support any military action in the war on terrorism. NYSPC made its stance on Iraq clear through its Web site, which stated, "The Bush administration is intent on plunging America into an illegitimate and preemptive war that will only increase danger for Americans and the world. At the same time education, health care, and the economy are being neglected."

On March 5, 2003, NYSPC organized one of the nation's largest student strikes, called Books Not Bombs. More than

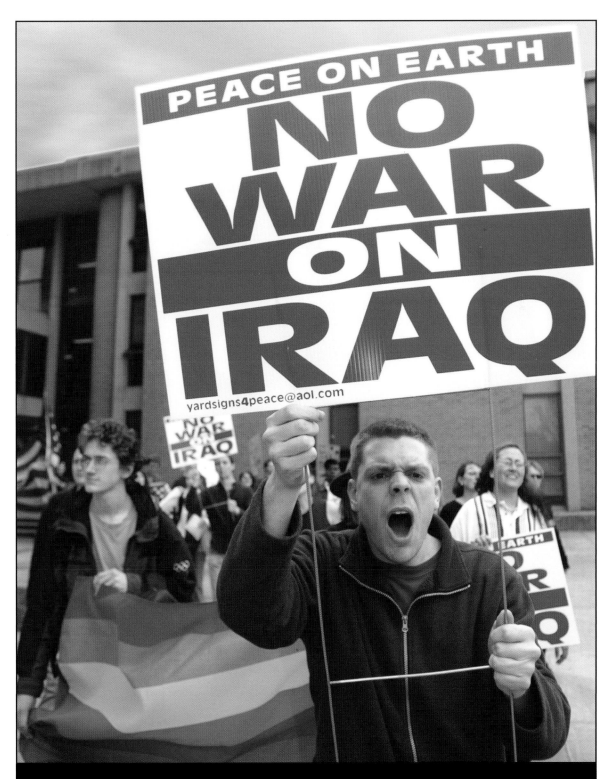

Students from the University of Tennessee shout antiwar slogans during a student-led protest.

300 U.S. campuses participated. Groups of students did different things at their protests. Many students left their classes to attend rallies. Other students staged sit-ins and die-ins or carried signs with messages such as "It's the Middle East, not the Wild West." Students in Vermont and Wisconsin protested at their state capitol buildings.

The Books Not Bombs movement was not limited to the United States. Five thousand Swedish students marched through Stockholm carrying signs that said "Stop the War" and "Fight U.S. Imperialism." In London, England, students staged a sit-in outside the home of Prime Minister Tony Blair. "We don't mean anything to Blair because we can't vote. But we will be able to soon, and he will pay the price for a war in Iraq," said a 16-year-old British protester.

Not all students were against the war, however, and many worked together to support the troops. In Greeley, Colorado, student Kate Novak set up a table in her high school's cafeteria to collect donations for the troops. The money was sent to the United Service Organization, which sent care packages to soldiers. The care packages contained items such as sunscreen, snacks, and calling cards.

Police remove a student who participated in a protest against the war in London's Parliament Square.

In St. Petersburg, Florida, students at Southside Fundamental Middle School also showed their support of the troops with a quiet ceremony. They said the Pledge of Allegiance and recited patriotic poems. The students also tied yellow ribbons to their lockers to represent their hopes that the troops would return home safely.

Not all demonstrators were against the war. This mother and son pray at a rally to show support for U.S. troops.

WORLDWIDE DAY OF PROTESTS

While there were protests in America, they took place all over the world as well. February 15, 2003, marked a worldwide day of protests. On this day, protesters around the globe voiced their opposition to the war. More than 600 protests took place.

The first massive antiwar protest of the day took place in Australia. Australia's government had supported President George W. Bush and even pledged to send 2,000 troops to the Middle East to help in the war. However, opinion polls in Australia showed that 33 percent of the country's people opposed going to war, no matter what.

As a result, more than 500,000 Australians protested the potential war with Iraq. At the protest, Bob Brown, of Australia's Green party, said, "This war is not Australia's war." Organizers said the turnout was the biggest antiwar protest since the Vietnam War. Peter Garrett, the former lead

NO WAR
The Greens

PEACE
NOT
R
NO WAR

AUSTRALIAN
LABOR
PARTY

NO WAR

ON IRAQ
OOPS HOME

he war coalition

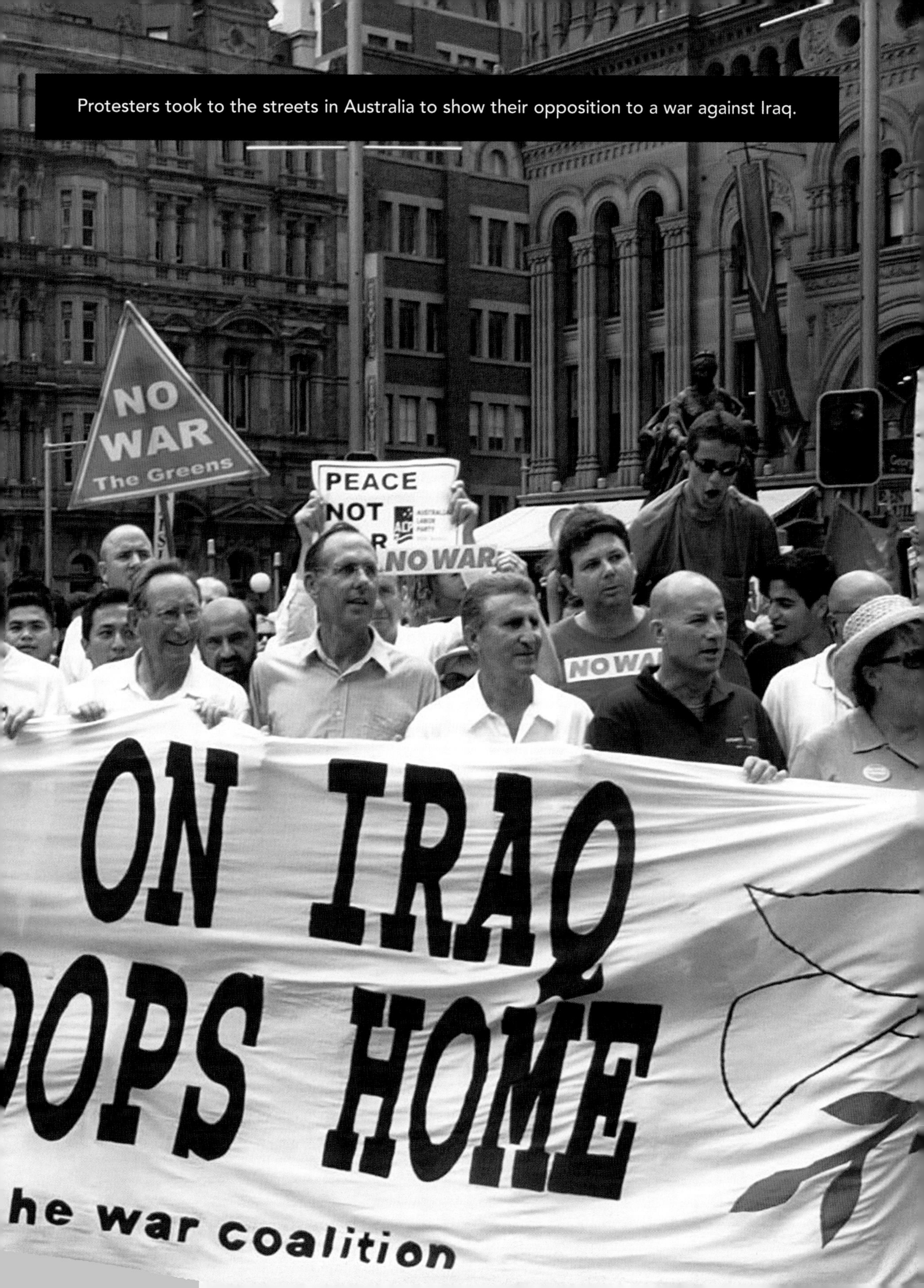

singer for the band Midnight Oil, was at the protest. He said, "We will bring together people from different political viewpoints and comprehensions, but they will be united because they have a strong sense of disquiet about what is going on."

The worldwide day of protests also reached Iraq. Tens of thousands of Iraqis protested in Baghdad, the nation's capital. Many of the men marched with machine guns in their hands, while women clutched pictures of Saddam. One of the banners carried through the crowd read "Our swords are out of their sheaths, ready for battle." Members of Saddam's ruling Baath party greeted the protesters.

People in other Middle Eastern countries also participated in the worldwide day of protests. In Syria's capital, Damascus, an antiwar protest took place. It was believed that 200,000 protesters participated, chanting anti-American and anti-Israeli sayings. In Israel, a group of 2,000 protesters marched in the city of Tel Aviv. The group was made up of both Israelis and Palestinians.

Protests were waged across Europe as well. At London's Hyde Park, an estimated 750,000 people demonstrated against the war. It was the largest protest ever to take place in London. Several British leaders spoke at the rally, including

Iraqis demonstrate in support of Saddam Hussein in Baghdad, Iraq.

London's mayor Ken Livingstone. "So let everyone recognize what has happened here today: that Britain does not support this war for oil. The British people will not tolerate being used to prop up the most corrupt and racist American administration in over 80 years," said Livingstone.

Many people in London protested the war, but others demonstrated their support. The most notable among them was British prime minister Tony Blair. "As you watch your TV pictures of the march, ponder this: if there are 500,000 on that march, that is still less than the number of people whose deaths Saddam has been responsible for," said Blair.

In other parts of Europe, people also took to the streets to show their opposition to the war. The two largest rallies took place in Rome, Italy, and Barcelona, Spain. Police reported that more than 1 million people showed up in each of these cities to protest the war. Millions of others protested in the Netherlands, Germany, France, and other parts of Europe.

The worldwide day of protests reached America, too. Police estimate that about 100,000 people demonstrated near the UN building in New York City. The group of protesters stretched down First Avenue for 20 blocks. One of the speakers at the protest was Nobel Peace Prize winner Archbishop

Antiwar protesters march in New York City.

Desmond Tutu. Tutu said, "We are members of one family, God's family, the human family. How can we say we want to drop bombs on our sisters and brothers, on our children?"

After the war began, worldwide protests continued. In Madrid, Spain, violence broke out between protesters and police on March 22, 2003. The protesters called for Spain's leader, José María Aznar, to resign because he supported the U.S. military action against Iraq. No one is sure why the violence at this protest began, but police responded by firing blanks, or shells with no bullet in them. Police also chased people through the streets of Madrid. Several arrests were made, and one police officer was injured.

On the same day in London, between 200,000 and 500,000 people marched against the war. They traveled through the city to Hyde Park. Protesters such as Andrew Murray, chairman of the Stop the War campaign, were angry that the war had started. They were also upset at the way the United States was treating the war. Murray said, "these slogans like 'Shock and Awe,' this Rambo-style rhetoric. Every bomb going off almost inevitably means dead civilians."

Protesters in Madrid, Spain, stage a die-in to protest against a proposed war against Iraq.

TWENTY-FIRST CENTURY PROTESTS

T he protests that took place across the globe in 2003 were different from any others in one important way. The organizers of the protests had sophisticated communications technology at their fingertips. They used this technology to organize their protests, as well as to organize virtual protests.

When groups decide to organize a protest, they work in a variety of ways to get their message out to the public. In the past, groups communicated through low-tech methods such as fliers, posters, phone calls, and letters. This required months of planning and labor. Though today's protesters still use these traditional methods, they also use new technology to reach more people faster than ever.

Many groups built their own Web sites, allowing visitors to the sites to quickly and efficiently find the dates, times, and locations of events. Many sites allowed visitors to make donations, read war updates, and even learn how to organize their own protests. In addition, mass email messages provided

thousands of protesters with logistical information, such as where to catch buses to a protest, in just seconds.

The use of this advanced technology is not limited to the United States. Shortly after the war began, protesters in Cairo, Egypt, used text messaging on cellular phones to organize 5,000 demonstrators. In Stockholm, Sweden, so many protesters were using their cell phones that the entire network crashed.

Protesters can also use technology itself as a means of protest. For example, thousands of Americans participated in a virtual march on February 26, 2003. It was organized by the group Win Without War, which is a coalition of 41 organizations.

In the virtual march, protesters did not actually march. Rather, they showed their opposition to the war in a different way. They flooded government offices with phone calls, faxes, and email messages. Win Without War's director, Tom Andrews, said the protesters generated more than 1 million phone calls and faxes. Organizers estimated that more than 400,000 people took part in the virtual march.

Win Without War

Advocating Alternatives to Preemptive War against Iraq
Keep America Safe

★ Artists United to Win Without War

★ American Friends Service Committee (AFSC)

★ American-Arab Anti-Discrimination Committee

★ Business Leaders for Sensible Priorities

★ Campaign for UN Reform

★ Conference of Major Superiors of Men

★ Council for a Livable World

★ Education for Peace in Iraq Center

★ Evangelical Lutheran Church in America

★ Families USA

★ Fourth Freedom Forum

★ Global Exchange

★ Greenpeace

★ Leadership Conference of Women Religious (LCWR)

★ MoveOn

★ Musicians United to Win Without War

★ NAACP

★ National Council of Churches

★ National Gay and Lesbian Task Force

★ National Organization for Women (NOW)

★ NETWORK A National Catholic Social Justice Lobby

★ Oxfam America

★ Pax Christi USA

★ Peace Action

★ Physicians for Social Responsibility (PSR)

★ Rainbow/Push Coalition

★ Shalom Center

★ Sierra Club

★ Sojourners

★ Soulforce

★ The Tikkin Community

★ TrueMajority

★ Unitarian Universalist Association of Congregations

★ United Church of Christ

★ United Methodist Church Board of Church and Society

★ Us Foundation

★ USAction

★ Veterans for Common Sense

★ Veterans for Peace

★ Women's Action for New Directions (WAND)

★ Working Assets

The organizations that form Win Without War

Actor Martin Sheen, right, stands with actor Robert Hall, left, to promote the virtual march on Washington, D.C.

BEYOND THE MARCHES

Taking part in large-scale marches is not the only way people showed their position on the war. People also found smaller ways to show their feelings, such as using yard signs. These signs had a variety of messages, ranging from "Say No to War With Iraq" to "Liberate Iraq: Support Our Troops."

Many groups also found other creative ways to get their points across. For example, some American protesters held candlelight vigils for peace. In Islamabad, Pakistan, protesters showed their unity by forming a human chain that spanned nearly six miles (10 km).

Throughout the world, people also looked to money as a way to protest. These protesters refused to buy American products. They hoped American companies would lose money, and then persuade President Bush to stop the attacks in Iraq.

In Germany, several restaurants took part in the boycott. They refused to sell American products such as Coca-Cola. Some restaurants even refused to accept American Express credit cards. "We want to hit America where it hurts—in their wallets. None of the customers have complained. On the contrary, most thought it was a great idea," said Fabio Angile, a restaurant owner in Berlin.

In the Middle East, consumers turned away from American goods, too. Restaurants such as McDonalds, Burger King, and Kentucky Fried Chicken reported low sales in Middle Eastern countries as tensions rose between the United States and Iraq. And consumers chose local products instead of American brands.

Other protesters showed their commitment to the antiwar cause by traveling to Iraq to act as human shields. Volunteers from Australia, Brazil, Israel, Spain, the United Kingdom, and the United States made the journey. As human shields, they hoped to guard schools and hospitals. They hoped coalition forces would not attack these targets if there were coalition citizens inside.

Instead, the Iraqi government deceived the human shields. They were not allowed to guard schools and hospitals.

Human shield peace activists gather inside the South Baghdad Power Plant.

They were told to guard oil refineries, water treatment plants, and power stations. These places were likely targets of a coalition attack, not the peaceful targets the human shields had hoped to protect. Angry that they had been lied to, most human shields returned home before the first attacks began.

As the war in Iraq drew to a close in May 2003, protesters continued to make their voices heard. But they had abandoned their antiwar demonstrations, and instead raised concerns over who would lead Iraq's new government. They wanted to make sure Iraqis, not Americans, governed the country. People of the world will continue to watch with interest. Undoubtedly, they will raise objections where they see injustice as a new era begins in Iraq's long and distinguished history.

WEB SITES
WWW.ABDOPUB.COM

To learn more about war protesters, visit ABDO Publishing Company on the World Wide Web at **www.abdopub.com**. Web sites about war protesters are featured on our Book Links page. These links are routinely monitored and updated to provide the most current information available.

Thousands of San Francisco citizens turned out to protest the possible war with Iraq.

TIMELINE

AUGUST 1990

Iraq invaded Kuwait

JANUARY 1991

January 15: UN forces called for Iraq to leave Kuwait by this date

January 16: Persian Gulf War began

SEPTEMBER 2001

September 11: al-Qaeda terrorists crashed airplanes into targets in New York City and Washington, D.C.

JANUARY 2002

January 29: George W. Bush called Iraq an "axis of evil" nation in his State of the Union address

NOVEMBER 2002

November 8: UN adopted Resolution 1441

JANUARY 2003

Protests erupted around the world, opposition to possible war with Iraq grew

FEBRUARY 2003

February 15: Worldwide antiwar protest day drew millions of people, largest groups protested in Europe and North America

February 26: Protesters launched a virtual march on Washington, D.C.

MARCH 2003

March 5: Thirty thousand students took part in the NYSPC's Books Not Bombs rally

March 17: Bush gave Saddam and his two sons 48 hours to leave Iraq, otherwise the United States would attack

March 19: Saddam remained in Iraq, the United States began its attack

March 27: A coalition of antiwar groups called M27 staged a die-in on a busy New York City street, reminding Americans of the people that would die in a war with Iraq

APRIL 2003

April 4: Friends of America rally held in Toronto, Canada

April 16: Violence ignited near European Union Summit, protesters angry over some nations' roles in the Iraqi conflict

FAST FACTS

- Iraqi deputy prime minister Tariq Aziz is the highest-ranking Christian in Iraq. Most people in Iraq are Muslims. The pope met with Aziz in an attempt to prevent war.

- The virtual march involved people placing phone calls, faxes, and email messages to their representatives in Congress. They did this to show they didn't like the war. Organizers claim that more than 400,000 people took part in the protest and that more than 1 million messages were sent to Congress.

- On March 17, 2003, war protesters in the United Kingdom appeared in London's International Petroleum Exchange. Their protest caused trading to stop for a short while.

- A protest in Madrid, Spain, on March 22, 2003, drew more than 100,000 people. The protesters held signs that read *No a la Guerra*. That is Spanish for No to the War. They didn't like Spanish president José María Aznar's support of U.S. president George W. Bush's military action in Iraq. The demonstration was a mile long.

- UN secretary general Kofi Annan criticized Iraq for using human shields in its country. He said Iraq should prevent people from putting themselves in danger.

- Most activists who came to Iraq as human shields believed they would be protecting schools or hospitals. Instead, the Iraqi government made them protect oil wells, water treatment plants, and power stations.

GLOSSARY

annex:
To add land to a nation.

civil disobedience:
Disobeying a law to protest something considered unfair or wrong.

dictator:
A ruler who has complete control and usually governs in a cruel or unfair way.

inevitable:
Something that cannot be stopped from happening.

logistics:
Planning the details of an event.

ultimatum:
A final offer that results in the use of force if rejected.

vigil:
An event in which people take time to come together and think about a particular action going on around them.

INDEX